Avoidant Attachment Recovery

Break Free from Avoidant Habits to Build Secure and Long Term Relationships

Linda Hill

Table Of Contents

Introduction

Have you ever entered a relationship where the other person seems uncomfortable with emotional closeness? Maybe you have experienced this yourself. You want to get close to your partner but cannot get yourself to do it. Just the thought of it makes you feel anxious.

I remember my relationship with men when I was younger. I wanted to be in a relationship, yet I always held back. I rarely initiated anything in my relationships, and I felt like leaving whenever I felt emotionally vulnerable. It was only years later that I learned that I had an avoidance attachment style.

If you ever wondered why the person you are with seems to keep their distance, it may have nothing to do with you. If you are the one who is having trouble getting close, I can reassure you that it is not your fault. I am saying this because the organizing principle behind this avoidance is subconscious, and its roots may have begun in childhood.

Attachment styles influence how we relate to others, especially in intimate relationships. These attachment styles were forged when we were infants and shaped by our relationship with our parents or caregivers. There are three major attachment styles, one of which is the avoidance attachment style. This attachment style leads to fear and mistrust of emotional intimacy. Though attachment styles are formed when we are very young, they often carry over to adulthood.

Though I have a strong background in psychology, I was unaware of the details of attachment styles until later in my life. As I studied attachment theory, I began to understand why I, and the people in my past, behaved the way they did. The experience of learning about attachment styles was very illuminating for me for these reasons, which is why I decided to write this book. I wanted to share this information with others. Though there are numerous other books on attachment styles on the market, I felt compelled to write this book because I know what it is like to have avoidant tendencies.

In this book, you find information about how the avoidant attachment style develops, how it impacts us, what it does to our relationships, and how you can move beyond the fears associated with it. As the avoidant attachment style does not exist in a vacuum, you will also find out about the other attachment styles and how they interact with the avoidant style. Whether you have an avoidant attachment style, or your partner does, this book can shed light on a relationship challenge that often leads to misunderstandings and hurt feelings. When there is light, there is an opportunity for growth and healing.

CHAPTER 1

What is an Attachment Style

When I was younger, I felt very insecure with men. Though I wanted to be in an intimate relationship, it scared me. I was afraid they would find out who the real me was and that I would be rejected. Because of this, I tried to keep things at the surface level. I did not show vulnerability and avoided getting involved in emotional encounters.

Though I was successful in keeping emotionally distant from my partners, I was never successful in my relationships. Because of my behavior, my relationships never lasted long. Most of them ended in less than a year. When my relationships ended, I always blamed myself. I felt that I was cursed. I wanted to be loved, but I was afraid of getting hurt. This created a vicious cycle. My lack of success in my relationships only reinforced my fears of being vulnerable.

Sometime later, I had to relocate to another state for work reasons. I did not know anyone except for my new co-workers. If I was not working, I would spend most of my time alone in my apartment. Though I have always spent my time alone, being alone this time was different.

My new environment caused me to reflect on my life. I began to realize that I was unhappy with how my life was going. I made the decision to see a counselor about my fears of becoming vulnerable with others. It was through therapy that I learned that I had an anxious attachment style. To understand what an anxious attachment style is, you first need to understand attachment theory.

In the 1930's psychologist, Harry Harlow did an experiment that helped pave the way to understanding attachment theory. I do need to point out that I find Harlow's experiment unethical, but it did provide insight into attachment styles.

In the experiment, Harlow took infant rhesus monkeys and separated them from their mothers. He then constructed two surrogate mothers. The first surrogate was constructed out of metal and had an artificial nipple from which the infant monkey could nurse. The second surrogate was made of a soft and fluffy material but did not provide nourishment.

When hungry, the baby monkeys went to the first surrogate. However, they went to the second one when they wanted comfort, as the second surrogate gave them a sense of security. When the baby monkeys were with the second surrogate, they were curious and explored their surroundings. When they encountered something, they were unsure of, they returned to the second surrogate.

When the infant monkeys were put in a new environment, without the second surrogate, they would not explore. Instead, they rocked back and forth on the floor and sucked on their thumb. Harlow's experiment demonstrated that the baby monkeys' need for comfort was just as important as nourishment. The second surrogate allowed the infant monkeys to build trust and confidence.

Harlow's experiment led to further study, including that of psychoanalyst John Bowlby. In 1969, Bowlby wrote his theory of human attachments. He believed that attachments were an instinctive emotional connection that made possible the exchange of care, comfort, and pleasure among individuals.

From an evolutionary perspective, Bowlby believed that attachments made it possible for the survival of our species. It was the attachment between mother and child that kept babies close to their mothers, thus, ensuring their survival. Bowlby identified four characteristics of attachments that make the relationship between parent and child meaningful:

Closeness: We desire to be near the person we have an attachment to.

Safety: The object of our attachment makes us feel safe.

Comfort: The comfort we get from our attachment figure gives us the confidence to explore our surroundings.

Separation Anxiety: We are anxious when our attachment figure is not around.

In the 1970s, Mary Ainsworth expanded Bowlby's studies by conducting her landmark study, the Strange Situation experiment. (Edward, 2017). In the experiment, Ainsworth investigated how children between 12-18 months responded when their mothers left them alone for brief periods.

In the experiment, a mother and her child were placed in a room alone. Ainsworth observed how willing the child was to explore while their mother was present. Later on in the experiment, a stranger would enter the room and briefly talk to the mother. The mother then would briefly leave the room, leaving the stranger with the child.

Based on her observations, Ainsworth created the three major attachment styles: Secure attachment, anxious attachment, and avoidant attachment.

The Attachment Styles

From the moment of our birth, we form attachments with our primary caregiver. These attachments became fully formed around the age of three.

The quality of the attachment that we formed with our primary caregiver determined our ability to trust others. As with the infant monkeys, having our emotional needs met allowed us to develop confidence, trust others, and explore the unfamiliar. However, if our emotional needs were not met, we did not develop the ability to trust others or explore the unknown.

Research has identified four different styles of attachments:

- Secure attachments

- Anxious attachments

- Avoidant attachments

If we had our emotional needs met as a child, we formed a secure attachment with our primary caregiver. We learned to trust others and build confidence within ourselves. The remaining attachment styles are based on fear, as our emotional needs were not met. They lead to anxiousness and mistrust of others. For this reason, they are known collectively as insecure attachment styles.

The attachment style that we developed as children may follow us into adulthood, which is knowing your attachment style can clarify your relationship challenges. The following is a brief explanation of the four attachment styles:

- **Secure Attachment Style:** You feel confident and recognize your self-worth. You can be open and supportive toward your partner.

- **Anxious Attachment Style:** You lack trust in your relationship and doubt your partner's feelings for you. As a result, you need constant reassurance from them.

- **Avoidant Attachment Style:** You fear becoming emotionally vulnerable and distance yourself in the relationship when there are feelings of emotional intimacy.

In the United States, an estimated 56% of the population has a secure attachment style, followed by 20% for the anxious style, 23% for the avoidant style, and 1% for disorganized (Hazen and Shaver, 1987). In the next chapter, we will take a deeper look at how attachment styles are created.

Note: The disorganized style will not be addressed in this book because of its rarity.

CHAPTER 2

How Did You Develop Your Attachment Style?

The previous chapter offered a brief explanation of how attachment styles are formed. In this chapter, we will take a deeper look into this. Attachments are lasting emotional connections between individuals. Through these connections, individuals seek security and closeness.

In adult-child relationships, attachments are developed by how the adult responds to the child's needs. Additionally, the attachment to the adult by the child is not based on the adult that spends the most time with them but rather by the adult that most meets the child's needs. The meeting of the child's need for a sense of security is the essence of attachment theory. The child needs to be able to find security when they feel threatened or unsure.

In the early 21st century, the National Research Council and the Institute of Medicine's Committee on Integrating the Science of

Early Childhood Development came to the following conclusion:

"Children grow and thrive in the context of close and dependable relationships that provide love and nurturance, security, responsive interaction, and encouragement for exploration. Development is disrupted without at least one such relationship, and the consequences can be severe and long-lasting." Their conclusion would shape their policies and practices. (Cassidy, Jones, and Shaver, 2013).

The Power of Connection

The fundamental premise of attachment theory is that a child's fears are lessened when they are in proximity to the person with whom they have formed an attachment. What creates trust in the child is the child's perception of the availability of that person to comfort them and make them feel safe. It is this perception that allows the child to determine if they can handle a perceived threat. If they feel they can handle a perceived threat, they will feel less anxiety and fear.

Even at a very early age, infants can take in complex information about the social interactions they observe. The information that is being referred to is both social and emotional in nature. In other words, infants can determine if the interactions that they witness are caring or adversarial.

Studies were done where puppets were used to demonstrate either supportive or adversarial relationships. The infants that observed the puppets were able to identify the kind of relationship the puppets had with each other. The infants showed a preference for those puppets that were supportive toward others. The researchers concluded that the infants knew what type of relationship the puppets should have with each other (Cassidy, Jones, and Shaver, 2013).

Knowing that they have someone who they can depend on for security not only benefits children emotionally, but it may also benefit them at a physiological level, which was demonstrated in a 1970s experiment. The experiment showed that there was a physiological response in infant rats when they were separated from their mothers. The rat pups demonstrated multiple changes in their physiological and behavioral levels. Body temperature, heart rate, food intake, and willingness to explore were all affected.

However, not all the rat pups responded in the same way. Rat pups that received the most attention from their mothers (in the form of maternal licking and grooming) were the least affected when separated. These pups also explored more than the other pups. Additionally, these differences were maintained into adulthood (Cassidy, Jones, and Shaver, 2013).

Attachment research conducted in 1996 showed that toddlers with an anxious attachment style had elevated cortical levels, a stress hormone, when introduced to new situations. The rise in cortical levels was also seen when mothers stopped interacting emotionally with their children. This change in cortical levels was also seen in children from violent homes, even when they were not directly exposed to the violence (Cassidy, Jones, and Shaver, 2013).

All evidence from the research points to the same thing. For healthy development, children need a caregiver that provides them with a sense of security, and they need to feel that they can depend on receiving that security when needed.

Internal Working Model of Attachment: Inside the Mind of an Infant

From the time they are born, children experience their primary caregivers. It is from these experiences that they form a mental representation of their relationship with them. In attachment theory, these mental representations are known as internal working models of attachment (IWM). IWM influences how children interact and form relationships with others. The child's expectations when interacting and forming relationships with others are based on their IWM.

A child's IWM is like a GPS or internal guidance system. It lays down the path for how the child will respond emotionally and behaviorally when interacting with others. This pathway can last throughout the child's lifetime unless there is a conscious decision to change.

The challenge is that these IWM operate beyond our conscious awareness, which is why changing them is difficult though possible. If not consciously addressed by the person, or there are no intervening events in the person's life, their IWM will remain operative throughout their lives. This is the reason why the quality of the parent-child relationship in the early stages of life is a strong predictor of the child's relationships when they become adults. Unless there is some form of intervention, IWMs can become intergenerational. Children with an avoidant attachment style are more likely to pass on this attachment style to their own kids when they become parents.

The Stages of Attachment Development

Bowlby identified four stages in the development of attachments, pre-attachment, attachment in the making, clear-cut attachment, and goal corrected.

The pre-attachment stage occurs between birth and two months. During this stage, the infant shows interest and is responsive to interactions with anyone they encounter. They have not yet developed an attachment to any single individual.

Because of this, they are not stressed if a loving and responsive caregiver takes over as the primary caregiver. What is important to the infant is that the person can comfort them.

Attachment-in-the-Making

This second stage occurs between the ages of two and six months. The infant starts to develop a preference for an individual caregiver. They express this through smiling and vocalizing. This is also the stage when infants become anxious when they encounter someone they do not know.

At this stage, the baby does not only develop an attachment with its primary caregiver but with others as well. This is also the stage when babies start to explore. While investigating their world, they keep an eye on their primary caregiver. It is the presence of the primary caregiver that gives the baby the confidence to explore.

Clear—Cut Attachment

This stage occurs between the ages of six months and two years and is marked by the child developing a strong attachment to their primary caregiver. They show signs of distress if separated from the primary caregiver for more than a brief period. In cases of prolonged separation, children may develop major trauma.

At this stage, the child's attachment to others is deeply

ingrained. The child has created IWMs of its relationships. As the child gets older, this internal model becomes more and more difficult to change. As our IWMs operate subconsciously, they become our experience of reality. We are unaware that our relationship issues are due to our attachment styles.

Goal-Corrected Partnership

This fourth stage occurs from age three to adolescence. This is the stage when the child's need to be with their primary caregiver becomes progressively less, given that the child knows where their caregiver is and their availability to them. This is also the stage when children learn that other people are separate individuals with their own personalities, thoughts, and desires.

At this phase, there is a transformation in the child's attachment relationships. The child's understanding of relationships changes from focusing on getting their needs met to the formation of reciprocal relationships. This is the stage where the child uses language to express their needs and is aware of space and time.

This is also the stage when children can benefit by engaging with others (other than the caregivers) regularly, as in the case of preschool. How children respond to their relationships with others will be shaped by the quality of attachments they form in the earlier stages.

What Shapes a Child's Attachment?

While there are stages to the development of attachments, there are also two factors that determine how a child's attachments will develop. Those two factors are quality and critical period.

Quality

Research shows a child's primary attachment figure is not based on how much time a person spends with the child but rather on the quality of the time that the person provides them. The primary attachment is the strongest form of connection for the child. However, the child also forms secondary attachments with those other than the primary attachment figures.

These additional attachments, also known as subsidiary attachments, vary in their level of intensity. A baby can form stronger attachments with people other than the primary caregiver if others provide a greater quality experience than the primary caregiver.

Critical Period

The critical period is the period when a child's early attachments are formed. During this time, the brain's plasticity is receptive to the influence of the attachment experience. When this period passes, the child's attachment pattern becomes deeply ingrained and is difficult to change.

Theories on Attachment Formation

So far in this chapter, you have learned about what attachments are, the stages of their formation, and the factors that shape them. But how are attachments formed? There are two theories regarding this, learning theory and evolutionary.

Learning Theory

Under the learning theory, all of our behaviors are learned as opposed to being innate or instinctual. Namely, a child is born as a blank slate. The child learns different behaviors through conditioning and association.

When a baby is fed by their mother, the baby learns to associate the mother with food. Conditioning can also be involved in behavior. The child learns that by engaging in a specific behavior, the child gets rewarded. An example of this is when a baby smiles, and their mother smiles back or kisses them.

Because the behavior (smiling) led to a favorable outcome, the baby will repeat this behavior in the future. Conversely, if the baby engages in a specific behavior that leads to a negative outcome, it will avoid repeating that behavior in the future.

Evolutionary Theory

While learning theory is based on the idea that our attachments to others come about through the process of learning, the evolutionary theory states that our attachments are hardwired within us from birth. Both Bowlby and Harlow (McLeod, 2017) believed that we are born preprogrammed to form attachments to others for survival purposes.

Under this theory, infants are born with the means to connect with others. These means come in the form of smiling, crying, and other behaviors that elicit nurturing responses from adults.

Based on this theory, attachments need to be formed within the first five years. If an attachment is not made within this period, the child will develop irreversible consequences to its development, such as increased aggression and reduced intelligence (McLeod, 2017). In the next chapter, we will take a deeper look into the different attachment styles. Though this book is about the avoidant attachment style, it is important to understand the other styles to create context.

CHAPTER 3

How to Determine Your Attachment Style

Before going into greater detail about the different attachment styles, read the following statements and see if any of them resonate with how you feel about yourself:

- "It is easy for me to connect with others. In my relationship with my partner, I have no problem depending on them. Also, I have no problem with them depending on me."

- "I am not happy with the level of emotional intimacy in my relationship. My partner is not as close to me as I would like them to be. Also, I often have doubts if they really love me."

- "I am not comfortable getting emotionally close to others, nor do I feel comfortable when they try to get close to me."

The first statement you read is what a person with a secure attachment may think. The second statement exemplifies the thinking of someone with an anxious attachment style, and the third statement reflects the thinking of someone with an avoidant attachment style. What follows is a more detailed look at each of the three styles.

Secure Attachment Style

Those with a secure attachment style tend to have healthy and long-lasting relationships. This attachment style was born out of a secure relationship with one's caregiver. In this kind of relationship, the child can freely express their need for validation or reassurance without fearing negative consequences.

In Ainsworth's experiment, she found that children who had a secure attachment exhibited the following:

- They were comfortable exploring the room while their mother was there.

- They went to their mother for comfort when they felt unsure.

- They greeted their mother with positive emotions when she returned to the room.

- They preferred being with their mother over a stranger.

The key to a secure attachment style is that the caregiver makes the child feel understood, valued, and safe. This is made possible because their caregiver is emotionally available for them. Additionally, the caregiver is self-aware. They are aware of their own emotions and behavior. The child learns from the caregiver and models their behaviors. Signs that you have a secure attachment style include:

- You can regulate your emotions.

- You readily trust others.

- You can communicate effectively.

- You can ask for emotional support.

- You are comfortable being alone.

- You are comfortable in close relationships.

- You can self-reflect on your relationships.

- You connect easily with others.

- You can manage conflicts.

- You have good self-esteem.

- You are emotionally available.

When you carry a secure relationship style into adulthood, you feel emotionally secure and can navigate relationships in a healthy way. You are also trusting, loving, and emotionally supportive toward your partners.

Anxious Attachment Style

Children develop an anxious attachment style when they learn that they cannot depend on their caregivers to meet their emotional needs. This attachment style comes from inconsistent parenting and not being attuned to the child's needs.

In this kind of child-parent relationship, the child does not feel a sense of security with their caregiver. The inconsistent parenting creates confusion for the child. In Ainsworth's experiment, children with this attachment style showed a high degree of distress when the mother left the room.

Inconsistent parenting is not the only way anxious attachment styles can form. This attachment style can also come from experiencing traumatic events or when parents are overly protective of a child. In this case, the child picks up on their parent's insecurity, which makes them fearful.

Those with an anxious attachment style may have had parents who:

- Were not consistent in comforting their child. Sometimes they may have comforted the child, while at other times, they were indifferent or detached.

- Were easily overwhelmed.

- Alternated between being attentive toward their child and pushing them away.

- Made their child feel responsible for how they felt, which may lead to the child becoming codependent later in life. The child grows up believing that they are responsible for other people's feelings (PscyhCentral).

Signs that you may have an anxious attachment style include:

- You are codependent.

- You have a strong fear of rejection.

- You depend on your partner for validation.

- You have clingy tendencies.

- You are overly sensitive to criticism.

- You have a need for validation from others.

- You have a problem with jealousy.

- You have difficulty being alone.

- You have low self-esteem.

- You feel unworthy of love.

- You have a strong fear of abandonment.

- You have issues with trust.

In relationships, your anxious attachment style may show up in the following ways:

- You feel unworthy of being loved and need continuous validation from your partner.

- You believe that they are responsible for the challenges in the relationship.

- You can become intensely jealous.

- Your low self-esteem causes you to distrust your partner.

- You are overly sensitive to your partner's behaviors and emotions. As a result, you jump to conclusions about your partner's intent.

These signs come from a strong fear of abandonment. Though you may want an intimate relationship, your fear of abandonment keeps you from developing the relationship you desire. Also, those with this attachment style may focus on their partner's needs at the expense of their own.

This attachment style can also develop in adulthood. This may occur if someone experiences inconsistent behavior from their partner. If a partner is inconsistent in expressing affection, or if they are emotionally abusive to them, the other person may develop anxiety or insecurity about the relationship. This often occurs in abusive relationships.

In an abusive relationship, a partner may constantly tell them that they are incompetent or stupid. Eventually, they may believe it. Because of this, they may cling to their partner. They rely on their partner to care for them because they do not believe that they can do it on their own.

Avoidant Attachment Style

The avoidant attachment style is formed when the caregiver of the child is strict, emotionally unavailable, or absent. The child does not feel supported, and they feel that they have been left to fend for themselves. Those who have an avoidant attachment style have difficulty forming long-term relationships as they fear emotional and physical intimacy.

As children, these individuals may have experienced the following:

- There was an expectation that they be independent before they were ready to be.

- They were punished for depending on their caregivers.

- They were rejected by their caregivers when they expressed their emotions or needs.

- Their basic needs were not a priority.

This kind of parenting does not always come from outright neglect. It may be that the parent was overwhelmed with other responsibilities. Regardless, the child grows up to be strongly independent and is uncomfortable looking toward others for support.

You may have an avoidant attachment style if you:

- You have a pattern of avoiding emotional or physical intimacy.

- You are fiercely independent.

- You avoid expressing your feelings.

- You have a dismissive attitude toward others.

- You cannot trust others.

- You feel anxious when others try to get close to you.

- You avoid interacting with others.

- You believe that you do not need others.

- You have commitment issues.

When they are in a relationship, individuals with this attachment style keep their distance; thus, there is a lack of emotional intimacy. The partners of those who have an avoidant attachment often feel like they do not know them and often feel stone-walled. In Ainsworth's experiment, children with the avoidant attachment style did not show a preference between their mother and the stranger. Also, they did not seek out comfort from their parent.

Important Note

Most people will not be an exact match for the profiles just described. The attachment styles cover a spectrum, so these profiles would only fit the most extreme cases. Normally, a person will show a mixture of attachment styles.

Attachment styles can only be determined by a trained professional. The purpose of this book is not to diagnose but rather to recognize unhealthy behaviors that may be interfering in your relationships so that you can address them.

Also, the attachment styles described are not intended to predict children's future behavior. Nor should it be inferred that our caregivers are responsible for our relationship challenges as adults. A child may begin life with anxious attachments but change for the better when they get older or vice versa.

There are numerous experiences that we have as we grow into adulthood that can influence our attachment styles. However, the attachment styles that we form as children can help predict our behavior later in life. Research shows that the best predictor of our attachment style as adults is the way we perceive our relationship with our parents and our parents' relationship with each other.

In the remaining chapters, we will explore the avoidant attachment style in greater detail.

CHAPTER 4

Avoidant Attachment Style

It is natural for us to crave love and affection and with good reason. From an evolutionary perspective, emotional intimacy is important for our development and growth, regardless of our age. Emotional intimacy allows us to share our thoughts and feelings with others. By connecting with others, we can support and reassure each other. Emotional intimacy allows us to feel recognized, valued, and appreciated. All these things help us feel emotionally safe.

Though they cannot articulate it, infants have a need for emotional intimacy. In fact, it is at this age that the foundation of emotional trust is forged. In their own way, the infant can determine whether they can trust and depend on their caregiver.

As with all attachment styles, the emotional availability of the caregiver is the determining factor for which attachment style the child will develop. The avoidant attachment style is created when the caregiver is largely emotionally unavailable to the child. The caregiver is not attuned to the child's emotional needs.

The child learns that the caregiver is not responsive to their needs. The caregiver has not responded to the child's cues, and the child gives up on getting the caregiver's attention. When the child does express emotions, it may elicit anger from the caregiver. Instead of expressing compassion and caring, the caregiver may become angry with the child because they want the child to become independent before it is age appropriate. As the child grows older, they adopt behaviors that allow them to meet their needs without connecting with others.

Caregivers who are likely to create an avoidant attachment in children are likely to be uncomfortable with displaying emotions, whether those emotions are positive or negative.

They may be physically present but devoid of the emotions to address the child's needs. The caregiver may be reserved and back off when the child seeks affection, support, or reassurance. It is not uncommon for such caregivers to have been raised by parents who treated them the same way.

From the time we are born, we are hardwired to desire emotional closeness. It is natural for the child to want to bond with the caregiver. After being persistently rejected by the caregiver, the child realizes they must go without the affection and attention they so profoundly desire. As a result, the child will suppress their need for emotional closeness and comfort. Psychology professor and distinguished scholar Jude Cassidy writes:

> "During many frustrating and painful interactions with rejecting attachment figures, they have learned that acknowledging and displaying distress leads to rejection or punishment." By not crying or outwardly expressing their feelings, they are often able to partially gratify at least one of their attachment needs, which is remaining physically close to a parent" (Catlett, 2022). These children learn they will not be comforted; they give up seeking closeness and no longer express their emotions.

As a result of such care giving, the child does not learn how to manage their emotions. They become distrustful of others and avoid emotional intimacy. It is this process that creates the avoidant attachment style. The following are examples of caregiver behaviors that may lead to the development of an avoidant attachment style:

- Ignoring the baby or child when they cry.

- Not expressing emotional reactions to the child's achievements or issues.

- Mocking the child for their concerns.

- Expressing annoyance at the child when they are experiencing problems.

- The avoidance of physical contact or touch.

- When the child is fearful or in distress, the caregiver may separate from the child physically.

- When the child is fearful or distressed, the caregiver becomes irritated with them.

- Shaming the child when they express themselves emotionally.

- Unrealistic expectations for the child to demonstrate independence when it is not age appropriate.

- Telling the child to "grow up," "stop acting like a baby," or "stop your crying" when the child expresses emotions.

- They ignore the child's cues that they are in distress.

Caregivers who are most likely to demonstrate these behaviors include those who:

- They were raised by parents with an avoidant attachment style.

- Are very young or inexperienced. They do not understand how to support their child.

- They have difficulty expressing empathy.

- Have a mental illness.

- Feel overwhelmed by parental demands.

- They are preoccupied with their career or demanding lifestyles.

It should be noted that these behaviors by the caregiver are not always intentional. Some caregivers who engage in such behaviors may want to do what is best for the child, but they do not know how, as their parents were distant from them. A mental illness such as depression can also prevent the caregiver from meeting the child's emotional needs.

Further, children exposed to such behaviors are not guaranteed to develop an avoidant attachment style. Factors such as the infant's unique emotional and behavioral characteristics and temperament may be behind this. Studies also show that some factors beyond caregiving practices can contribute to children developing this attachment style; such factors include traumatic events and life experiences such as a parent's death, divorce, parental illness, and adoption (Catlett, J., 2022).

While emotionally unavailable caregivers can cause the avoidance attachment style, this attachment style can also develop from an emotionally enmeshed environment. In enmeshed homes, there is a lack of personal boundaries and minimal privacy, if any. This kind of environment commonly leads to depression, fear, anxiety, guilt, shame, and grief. These conditions can lead to children having difficulty identifying and expressing their feelings, thus becoming emotionally unavailable (MacWilliam, 2022).

The Two Kinds of Avoidant Attachment Styles

There are two kinds of avoidant attachment styles, fearful and dismissive. These two types differ in how they respond to others.

Fearful-Avoidant vs. Dismissive

Fearful avoidants tend to withdraw from emotional intimacy out of fear, while dismissive avoidants have a disregard for the need to connect with others.

Individuals who have fearful avoidance generally have low self-esteem, along with being very anxious. They do not believe that they are worthy of love. Those with a dismissive avoidant style have a very high level of self-esteem and low levels of anxiety. They have a very positive self-image.

Of the different insecure attachment styles, those with the

fearful-avoidant type have greater emotional challenges. They are more likely to experience depression and be less assertive. Also, they may appear to behave in ways that seem confused, aimless, or contradictory when feeling stressed.

Those with a dismissive avoidant style come across as being cold, and they tend to view others in a negative way. They do not feel a need to gain the acceptance of others and view others who seek emotional support as being weak. In fact, they often do not view relationships as being necessary.

Avoidant Attachment Style vs. Avoidant Personality Disorder

Unlike avoidant attachment style, avoidant personality disorder is a personality disorder. We all have personality traits; some of us are shy, while others are extroverts. Being shy is not a disorder because it does not prevent the person from functioning day today, nor is it a significant source of stress.

Having an avoidant personality can be debilitating as it can prevent day-to-day functioning and be a significant source of stress. Avoidant personality disorder is one of the more severe personality disorders, as it can lead to severe social dysfunction. While the avoidant attachment style does not lead to avoidant personality disorder, avoidant personality disorder may be associated with an avoidant attachment style.

Common Characteristics of Avoidant Style Attachment in Children

Children with an avoidant attachment style may exhibit the following characteristics:

- They are resistant to being comforted by their caregivers.

- They seem to be very independent.

- They seem to not desire nurturance or affection.

- While they will seek to be near their caregiver, they avoid having contact with them.

Another characteristic of an avoidant style in children is that they withhold the expression of their distress. In Chapter 2, there was a mention of Ainsworth's "strange situation" experiment. As a reminder, the children with the avoidant attachment style appeared to remain calm when the caregiver left the room. When the caregiver returned, the child avoided contact with them.

From their outward appearance, these children seemed to be

calm; however, this is deceiving. When their physiological responses were measured, these children showed the same level of distress as those with secure attachments. Children with an avoidant style suppress their fears (Li, 2022).

Avoidance Attachment Style in Adults

Adults with the avoidance attachment style appear confident, independent, self-directed, and self-assured. They give the appearance of being in control of their lives. Since they avoid emotional intimacy, they often focus on their careers. For this reason, they may be very successful.

They also may have a lot of friends, sexual partners, and acquaintances, and they can be fun to be with. Because they do not seek emotional support, their connections with others remain superficial. The following are signs that an adult may have an avoidance attachment style. They tend to:

- Avoid physical touching and eye contact.

- Do not ask for help.

- May have unusual eating habits.

- Have difficulty sharing their emotions or feelings.

- Accuse their partners of being over-attached or too clingy.

- Do not accept emotional support from others.

- Avoid intimacy out of fear of getting hurt.

- Choose personal independence over relationships.

- Do not allow their partner to rely on them.

- Appear calm in highly emotional situations.

In addition to these signs, adults with this attachment style may use other strategies to manage their emotions and feel safe. These include:

- Choosing not to get closer in a relationship out of fear of rejection.

- Redirecting their gaze from sights that make them uncomfortable.

- Tuning out during conversations about attachment issues.

- Suppressing their memories of negative events that involved their attachment issues. Further, it is common for these individuals to have few memories of their childhood relationships with their parents.

- Placing much of their focus on themselves and their creature comforts.

- Showing a disregard for the interests or feelings of others.

- Because they resist sharing their feelings, their response to conflicts is to become aloof and distant.

Adults with this attachment style tend to have an inflated view of themselves while having a cynical or negative attitude toward others. Their inflated view of themselves is a defensive strategy to protect their sense of self, which is extremely vulnerable and fearful of rejection. At a deep level, these individuals experience low self-esteem and feelings of self-hatred. They will often react with anger when they feel that their false image is being attacked.

The Advantages of Having an Avoidant Attachment Style

Those with an avoidant attachment style miss out on meaningful and fulfilling relationships; however, having this attachment style has its advantages.

Workplace Advantages

A study (Frankenhuis, 2010) theorized that insecure attachment styles (anxious and avoidant) might have an evolutionary significance. These attachment styles comprise 33 50% of the world's population and are most highly concentrated in areas with instability and poverty. The study points out that while these attachment styles cost the individual, they may benefit the group.

According to the theory, those with an avoidant attachment style have the makeup that allows them to respond to threats quickly and independently, thus increasing the chances of survival for the group members. Because of their sensitivity and quick detection of threats, those with anxious attachment styles are specially equipped to detect threats, which also serves the group.

The abilities of those with insecure attachments carry over to the workplace. The study showed that those with an avoidant attachment style serve the workplace with increased productivity while saving resources. Workers with an avoidant attachment style can quickly identify a workplace issue and either resolve it or reduce its impact.

Also, avoidant-style employees require less support from others. They are very independent and confident in their abilities and decision-making. These factors, plus the fact that they do not desire to socialize with others, make them more efficient at work while reducing the demand for resources.

Also, this attachment style is more likely to be success-driven. Their focus is on work rather than a social life, so they frequently achieve greatness in their careers.

Relationships

Though there can be many relationship challenges with this attachment style, these individuals offer the benefit of being less needy or demanding than the other attachment styles. Further, they tend to be more respectful toward others' boundaries. They will also be more respectful toward their partner's freedom.

Those with an avoidant attachment style tend to be very popular and sociable. They are very confident in social situations because emotional closeness is not involved. This is why this attachment type tends to have many friends instead of close relationships.

Additionally, these individuals are a great source of practical advice as they are guided by logic rather than emotion. For this reason, they are very honest. They will tell you what you need to hear instead of what you want to hear.

In the next chapter, we will take a deeper look into how relationships are affected by this attachment style.

CHAPTER 5

How an Avoidant Attachment Style Affects Relationships

Do you have doubts about ever finding that special person with whom you want to share your life with? Maybe you found yourself following a pattern of having relationships with partners who are emotionally unavailable. You may have started to doubt yourself and wondered if there was wrong with you. If this describes you, there may be a deep-seated reason for why you are experiencing this.

Having a romantic relationship with someone who has an avoidant attachment style is anything but easy. Honestly, not many people can make it work, as it can be a very frustrating and unsatisfying experience. Emotional intimacy in a relationship can only happen when both partners are willing to be vulnerable and communicate their thoughts and feelings.

The partner who has an avoidant attachment style tends to perceive relationships as emotionally draining and stressful. This should not be a surprise, as one of the traits of this attachment style is to be fiercely independent.

As a result, they will frequently feel resentful or uncomfortable when their partner turns to them with emotional needs. Those with an avoidant attachment style want to avoid having to navigate emotions. Because they avoid experiencing emotions, they have little self-awareness of what they are feeling. This is why they feel so easily overwhelmed by the emotional needs of others.

When the partner with this attachment style experiences their own negative emotions or they are put in a situation where they must experience the emotions of their partner, their defenses go up. They will distance themselves from their partner, either physically or emotionally. The following are some examples of distancing behaviors:

- If the partners live together, they will isolate themselves in certain areas of the home.

- They will avoid physical closeness, be it holding hands or sex.

- They will not make future commitments.

- They will not say that they love you.

- They will not listen to or validate their partner's feelings.

- They will walk ahead or behind their partner.

- They will dismiss their partner's feelings, including legitimate frustrations.

- They may engage in addictive behaviors such as sex, gambling, substance abuse, or pornography.

The partner of the avoidant personality is likely to feel confused as they cannot understand them, which leaves them not knowing what to do or think. One of the reasons why partners feel so confused is that the avoidant attachment style, and other insecure attachment styles, have not been covered as widely by the media. Unlike other disorders, such as narcissism, this attachment style has not received nearly as much attention.

If information on this and other insecure attachment styles were more widely available, it would help clear up the confusion of their partners. When this occurs, partners would realize that their partner's behavior is not the result of anything they did. Rather it is part of their partner's emotional dysfunction.

The defense mechanism of this attachment style is to avoid emotional intimacy with their partner, particularly when they are feeling stressed. If the thinking of the avoidant attachment personality could be summed up in one line, it would be: "We coexist, but you do you, and I will do me." The best partner for this attachment style is a person who is satisfied with being in a romantic relationship without much emotional intimacy.

If you are very independent, do not desire much communication or emotional sharing, and are content with your present circumstances, then you might find this kind of relationship satisfying.

As children, the bonding experience that we had with our caregivers was our first relationship. That relationship influenced how we related to intimacy later in life. The three attachment styles can provide insight into not only our behavior but our partner's. Understanding this can help us understand our needs and how to handle the challenges we experience. This is particularly true if a person who has an avoidant attachment style enters a relationship with someone who has an anxious attachment style.

When Avoidant and Anxious Meet

At an unconscious level, we may select partners that respond to us as our caregivers did. Further, how we behave in intimate relationships may be governed by our expectations, which originated from our childhood experiences. In other words, our attachments can cause us to behave toward our partners in the same way we act toward our caregivers.

Are you attracted to someone who may have an avoidant attachment style? If you do, you may consider doing some self-reflection as it may indicate that you have an anxious attachment style. Generally, we end up in relationships with those who validate our pre-existing beliefs regarding relationships.

The outcome is predictable when an anxious style gets into a relationship with an avoidant style. When the avoidant style is stressed, they will distance themselves from their partner. By distancing themselves, the avoidant partner can gain the independence and autonomy needed to regulate their emotions and deal with their distress.

The challenge is that the anxious style partner feels rejected and threatened by feelings of abandonment. In response, they strive to regain their connection with their partner. As their partner is of the avoidance type, they feel even more threatened.

Anxious Attachment Style

The person with an anxious attachment style may be clingy in their relationships; they have a continuous need for attention and love. They also may feel emotionally drained by their ongoing concern about whether their partner really loves them. Other characteristics of the anxious attachment style include:

- You desire closeness and intimacy with your partner, but you are held back by your lack of trust that they will be there for you.

- Your intimate relationship is all-consuming, and it is your primary focus.

- You lack boundaries for yourself and often violate your partner's boundaries.

- Your partner's wish for space threatens you. It may cause you to experience fear, panic, or anger. These feelings only reinforce your fear that your partner is no longer interested in you.

- Your self-esteem is determined by how you feel your partner is treating you.

- You jump to conclusions or overact when you perceive a threat to the relationship.

- You feel anxious when you are not with your partner. Also, you may become controlling or try to make them feel guilty as a way to keep them close to you.

- You seek constant reassurance from your partner.

- Friends or family may tell you that you are clingy or needy.

Those with this attachment style follow a predictable relationship pattern. The early stages of the relationship are marked by excitement and anticipation of what the relationship could become. There is that first kiss and the anticipation for when they can be with the other person. This stage is common in many relationships, and it has an almost addictive quality as there is a release of dopamine.

With time, the relationship begins to level out. This stage of the relationship is also normal, but it is threatening to the person with an anxious attachment style. This person may start to wonder if their partner has lost interest in them.

This sense of doubt puts their partner in a losing position. Even if their partner tries to reassure them, the person with this style of attachment will never be satisfied. They will continue to believe that their partner is losing interest in them. They may have thoughts like:

- Why does my partner not desire me the way that I desire them?

- Why have they not called me? I have not heard from them all day.

- I need to be more attentive to them, and then they will desire me more.

Unlike the authentic bond enjoyed by those with a secure attachment, those with an anxious attachment try to fulfill a bond that is built on a fantasy. Instead of experiencing genuine love, their bond is based on an emotional hunger. They are looking for a partner to rescue them from their own feelings of inadequacy. This usually causes their partner to back away.

Avoidance Attachment Style

Individuals with an avoidance attachment style are fearful of emotional intimacy. For them, freedom and independence are what is most important to them. They feel threatened by intimacy and closeness within a relationship. The following are examples of how this attachment style affects a romantic relationship:

- A person with this attachment style will be very independent and not feel that they need anyone.

- They will pull away if their partner tries to get close to them.

- They are uncomfortable expressing their emotions. If their partner tells them that they are being distant, they will tell their partner that they are being needy.

- They will be dismissive of their partner's feelings.

- They may have affairs as a way to reclaim their sense of freedom.

- They feel more comfortable with temporary or casual relationships than intimate and long-term ones.

- Intellectually, they believe that they do not need intimacy. In their hearts, however, they do desire a close and meaningful relationship.

- They focus on their own needs as they do not feel safe turning to their partner for help. This often leads to a no-win situation, so they do not get their needs met.

The partner with the anxious attachment style craves emotional intimacy but fears it because they are afraid of getting hurt. Further, they do not trust that their partner loves them. The partner with the avoidant attachment style is fearful of emotional intimacy, so they distance themselves. This behavior by the avoidant partner consists of the expectations of the anxious partner. The anxious partner has an expectation that their partner will not be emotionally vulnerable, and the partner with the avoidant attachment style plays this role perfectly.

Attachment Styles and Sex

Attachment styles affect all aspects of the relationship, and that includes sex. When an anxious-styled partner enters a relationship with an avoidant partner, both will be sexually unsatisfied.

Avoidant Attachment Style and Sex

Those with an avoidant attachment style are more likely to engage in casual sex than to develop a loving relationship. This is understandable, given that this attachment style avoids showing emotions. Because of this, they tend to get involved in short-term relationships, engage in casual sex, or not have sex at all.

Instead of intimacy, those with this attachment style are more likely to resort to pornography or emotionless sex. Since sex involves closeness, both physically and psychologically, sex makes them uncomfortable. Rather than being driven by passion and affection, they are sexually driven by their egos. For them, sex is a way to reduce stress, gain status with their peers, or control or manipulate their partners.

Anxious Attachment Style and Sex

Those with an anxious attachment style commonly have an unsatisfactory sex life. This is due to the characteristic behaviors that accompany this attachment style. Individuals with this style excessively worry about what others are thinking about them.

They have a strong fear of being rejected. Additionally, any perceived lack of interest by their partner can cause them to become emotional. Also, they feel misunderstood or not appreciated by their partners. All of this can be a put-off for their partners.

The sexual behavior of those with an anxious attachment style is usually driven by their feeling of a lack of love or security. Because of this, their sexual experiences are unfulfilling. This attachment group is likely to have more sexual partners than other attachment styles. They are also more likely to be unfaithful to their partners. Their motive to engage in sex is often to get their partner's attention, reassurance, and approval.

Avoidant Attachment Style and Work Relationships

Within the last five years, researchers have been paying more attention to how attachment styles play out in the workplace. One study (Hazen and Shaver, 1990) involved the social dynamics of attachment theory in the workplace. Their findings are as follows:

Avoidant Attachment Style in the Workplace

Unsurprisingly, those with an avoidant attachment style have no interest in team building or improving their relationship with their co-workers or managers. In fact, they may have a cynical view of those they work with. These workers have distrust for others and prefer to work alone. The challenge these workers pose to the workplace is that they are not likely to conform to the rest of the group and may be critical and resistant toward their superiors. These are the workers that are most likely to be the troublemakers.

The benefits to the workplace that this attachment style brings are that they tend to respond effectively and without hesitation to workplace threats. Further, they enhance the focus and productivity of their workgroups and are the ones most likely to meet their deadlines (Lavy, Bareli, and Ein-Dor, 2014)

CHAPTER 6

How to Cope with an Avoidant Attachment Style

None of the insecure attachment styles are a form of mental illness. As with the other insecure attachment styles, the avoidant attachment style was adopted during childhood as a way to cope with not getting one's emotional needs met.

The avoidant attachment style served its purpose when it was needed. The challenge is that retaining this adaptation as one grows older poses many challenges. Overcoming an avoidant attachment style involves learning new ways of thinking that support one's happiness and being able to connect with others. Though this may sound simple, making such a change takes patience, determination, and persistence.

Making such a change can be difficult and scary because it requires learning to trust oneself and others, both of which go against the way avoidant attachment styles were programmed.

However, it can be done! As healthier ways of viewing oneself sink in, the corresponding behaviors and emotions will follow.

Creating Change

Each of us has the potential to create change in our lives, regardless of age. Though our attachment styles are the result of deep-seated beliefs, we can change them. Creating a change in our beliefs requires that we challenge them. To do so, however, requires support, practice, and patience. The reason for this is our self-talk, our harshest critic, will resist our attempts to change.

This voice was developed from our childhood experience and will do its best to keep us from experiencing our emotions. It is the experiencing of emotions that the insecure attachment styles are designed to save us from.

Fortunately, recognizing one's insecure attachment style is half the battle in creating change. There can be no healing without self-awareness. Understanding one's attachment style lets one know what one must work on. Developing a more secure attachment style is definitely possible regardless of one's insecure attachment style.

Ways to Cope with an Avoidance Attachment Style

There is hope for those with an avoidant attachment style to develop a more secure attachment style within a relationship. However, as with all insecure attachment styles, it is important to clarify that this does not mean that someone with an avoidant attachment style can change into a secure attachment style. Rather, the individual learns to recognize their triggers and respond to them in a more empowering way.

Reflecting on Intimacy

The foundational challenge for the avoidant attachment style is the fear of emotional intimacy. It is here that one's efforts must focus because the switch for turning on intimacy has been on the off position since childhood. Coping with this attachment style involves learning to turn that switch on again. To begin with, you can ask yourself the following questions:

- What emotional and physical sensations do I experience when I think about becoming emotionally intimate with someone?

- What do I need emotionally to feel safe? Answering this question will involve exploring and understanding your needs and the ability to express them to others.

- What can I do to build closer relationships with others?

The point behind this question is to create and follow a step-by-step process for allowing others in and dealing with the emotional needs of those close to you.

The following are suggestions for overcoming the avoidant attachment style within an adult relationship:

Face Your Inner Critic

When working to overcome any of the insecure attachment styles, the most challenging opponent you will face is your inner critic, more commonly known as your self-talk. This critical voice was formed in early childhood. Unless we bring our awareness to this voice, we will continue to do its bidding.

It is this inner voice that creates distrust of others, and that warns us that we will be criticized or judged if we express our emotions. Those of us who have an avoidant attachment style use this self-talk to self-regulate our emotions. On the other side of the coin, this voice may be overly protective of us. It may be telling us grandiose thoughts about ourselves to distract us from feelings of lack of self-worth.

To challenge your self-talk, first, spend time identifying the thoughts that you experience regarding emotional intimacy. When you identify these thoughts, challenge them. You can do this by looking for evidence in your life that disproves this thinking. You can then learn to agree to disagree with your self-talk. The following is an example:

You think: "I will not get into a relationship; they will just let me down."

To counter that thought, think of a time when someone in your life was there for you. If you can do this, you will prove your inner critic wrong in this instance.

Honoring Your Need for Personal Space

We all need personal space; however, this is even more true for those with an avoidant attachment style. Having personal space is a must for these individuals as it allows them to ground themselves when stressed, allowing them to feel safer in the relationship.

Know Who to Trust

A major part of overcoming this attachment style is learning to trust others. However, not everyone is trustworthy. For this reason, it is helpful to determine the trust level of those around you. One way to do this is to share with another person some information that is inconsequential to you. If you see that the other person responds respectfully and does not tell others, you will be more likely to trust them with more meaningful information.

Develop Your Communication Skills

For a relationship to be fulfilling and successful, both partners must be open about their thoughts and feelings. For those with this attachment style, sharing their thoughts and feelings is terrifying. For them, it means exposing themselves to potential rejection or criticism. It is also about feeling out of control. For this reason, these individuals must learn to share their feelings in a manner where it feels safe for them, and they are in control.

Both partners must be able to express themselves honestly and openly. By doing this, each partner helps the other regulate their emotions. For this to happen, both partners must strive to communicate clearly to express their concerns without the fear of being judged.

When expressing your thoughts and feelings, pay attention to the physical sensations and thoughts that arise as you do so. In time you will realize that sharing your feelings with others is more enjoyable and healthier than denying them or repressing them.

Imagine that you are talking to your partner, and you sense that it is about to become an argument. It would be normal for an avoidant attachment style to avoid rising emotions by withdrawing from the situation either mentally or physically. Either way, your partner will feel like you are disregarding their concerns.

Instead, here is something that you could say that would honor both of you: "I see things are getting heated right now. Why don't we take a break for a few minutes and continue talking afterward?" If you are in a situation where you need to have some space, you could tell your partner:

- "I appreciate you for always being there for me. I need some space. I promise to discuss your concerns when I am ready."

- "I get how important it is for us to discuss this, but I need time to myself to clear my head. Can we discuss this later? I will be in better shape to talk about it then."

- "We have so much going for us as a couple. Why don't we take a breather and continue this discussion later?"

Therapy

Probably the most effective way to overcome your attachment style is through therapy from a professional who is experienced with working with insecure attachment styles. Studies have demonstrated that therapy can effectively work with avoidant attachment styles (WebMD, 2021).

A good therapist can provide an environment where you can feel safe exploring and expressing your thoughts and feelings. Further, a therapist can help you identify your attachment triggers and how to manage your emotions.

A therapist can help you explore your experiences of the past. By doing so, you will be able to realize what is specifically preventing you from experiencing meaningful relationships and interactions. You can then determine what changes you want and create a plan for accomplishing these changes.

Another reason therapy is so valuable in changing one's attachment style is that it becomes a model for a healthy relationship. It's a safe place to express one's thoughts and feelings. Further, it provides the opportunity to learn new skills for reducing anxiety when talking about topics that are important to you. The following kinds of therapies help deal with avoidant attachment styles in adults:

- Cognitive behavioral therapy (CBT)

- Schema therapy

- Narrative therapy

- Couples therapy

- Psychodynamic therapy

Cognitive Behavioral Therapy (CBT)

CBT is a form of therapy that is effective for treating a variety of issues, including anxiety disorders, depression, eating disorders, and substance abuse. There are numerous scientific studies that demonstrate CBT's effectiveness. CBT differs from many other forms of therapy in that it sees psychological issues as being caused by limited or negative thinking. It also has the following philosophies:

- Psychological issues are based on patterns of behaviors that we learned.

- If you are experiencing psychological issues, you can learn better ways of coping with them, which will lessen symptoms and allow you to become more effective in life.

In CBT, you learn new strategies to:

- Recognize the distorted thinking that is causing your problems and modify your thinking so that it supports you.

- Understand your motivations and the motivations of those around you.

- Learn how to increase your self-confidence in your abilities.

- How to challenge your fears instead of running away from them.

- Learn how to handle difficult interactions through role-play.

- Learn how to relax and calm your mind and body.

Schema Therapy

In psychology, schema is a term for a thought pattern that leads us to engage in unhealthy behaviors or relationship issues. Schemas normally develop in childhood as the result of not getting one's emotional or physical needs met. For this reason, schema therapy is another method for dealing with an avoidant attachment style.

In schema therapy, you will learn to recognize your thought patterns and behaviors that lead to avoidant behavior and learn how to change them. You will also learn more effective ways of coping with relationship challenges. Unlike CBT, there has not been enough research in schema therapy to determine its effectiveness.

Narrative Therapy

Narrative therapy involves realizing the story that you tell yourself, which influences your life. Going through life, you have numerous experiences to which you give meaning. The meaning that you give to these experiences becomes your story. As you go through life, you bring your story with you. This story gives meaning to the experiences you will have in the future and in how you see the world.

A therapist will help you in putting together your narrative.

Putting together a narrative allows you to create distance between you and your challenges so that you can see them more clearly.

Narrative Therapy can help with attachment issues, anxiety, depression, grief, and more. Also, there is no judgment, as the client is the expert.

Couples Therapy

Couples therapy is psychotherapy that focuses on helping improve relationships. If you are experiencing relationship challenges, couples therapy can help resolve those issues and rebuild the relationship. Also, couples therapy can be helpful at any stage of a relationship.

If you or your partner has an avoidant attachment style, couples therapy can help you and your partner understand each other better, improve communication skills, and deal with dysfunctional behaviors. The therapist has a range of therapeutic skills, one of which is emotionally focused therapy (EFT). The effectiveness of EFT has been supported by research.

Psychodynamic Therapy

A form of talk therapy, psychodynamic therapy involves talking to a therapist about your challenges, which can lead to feelings of relief and coming up with solutions. Psychodynamic therapy can help you better understand your thoughts, feelings, and motivations.

With a greater realization of your emotional patterns, you will become more effective in problem-solving and or managing your behavior. Psychoanalysis can be used to treat:

- Anxiety

- Depression

- Interpersonal problems

- Social anxiety disorders

- Post-traumatic stress disorder

- Substance abuse

Helping Children with an Avoidant Attachment Style

Helping children with this attachment style takes a two-prong approach. The first approach is directed at the caregiver by offering them education and support. Additionally, family therapy may also be used to help family members communicate more effectively and give them the tools to have more positive interactions with each other. In such cases, the therapy takes place in the person's home.

In the second approach, the therapist works directly with the child with the avoidant attachment style. The therapy aims to help the child develop a sense of self-worth, express their emotions, show empathy, and trust others. The therapy normally involves play therapy and can include puppets, storytelling, and art therapy.

Through such therapy, the child learns to overcome the avoidant attachment style's thoughts, behaviors, and feelings. Ultimately, such therapy is beneficial because it provides the child with a safe environment to try new behaviors and explore their emotions.

CHAPTER 7

Dating and Relationships with a Partner who has an Avoidant Style Attachment

In this chapter, you will find information about dating and relationships with someone who has an avoidant attachment style. We will begin with signs to look out for when dating that may indicate that the other person has an avoidant personality.

Signs that Your Date May Have an Avoidant Style

Imagine that it is your first date and that it is going great. You and your date are enjoying each other's company, and the conversation is flowing. Everything points to the possibility that this may be the beginning of something great.

By the end of the next day, you had not heard from your date. You start getting an uneasy feeling and decide to call them.

When you talk to them, they seem distant. When the phone call ends, you are left with nothing to make you feel better about the situation. Before you start thinking that maybe it is something that you did, consider the possibility that your date has an avoidant attachment style.

The following signs may indicate that your date has an avoidant attachment style:

They Do Not Reach Out to You

When you spend time together, they seem to be enjoying themselves, but they never say anything about what it means to them to be with you.

The reason for this is that those with this attachment style want to feel love and connection, but they are afraid to experience these feelings. As a result, they have a compulsive need to distance themselves when they start to experience these feelings. They feel triggered by feelings of emotional intimacy because it leaves them feeling vulnerable to rejection or abandonment.

They Seem Uneasy When You Show Negative Emotions

Those with this attachment style have been conditioned since birth to associate the expression of negative emotions with fear and anxiety. Because they received inconsistent parenting, they have learned that reaching out to others may lead to rejection or abandonment.

You may be expressing negative emotions about something that has nothing to do with your date. However, they may get triggered as though they were the target of your emotions. In other words, they will feel like they are being attacked.

It may seem like they are just not interested in having a serious conversation when, in fact, they are reacting to fear. If you express negative emotions regarding their behavior, they may become defensive as they fear rejection or abandonment at a subconscious level.

They Do Not Ask You for Help or for Favors

Those with an avoidant attachment style are fiercely independent due to their fear of rejection. They are constantly anticipating that they will be disappointed. On the same token, they also do not want anyone looking toward them for help.

Those with this attachment style will often not offer support or help to others when they reach out to them. The reason for this is that they equate offering help or doing favors with making themselves vulnerable. This feeling goes back to when they were being raised and when they were met with rejection when they reached out to their caregivers. If they do a favor for you, they will downplay its meaning. They may even feel irritated if you express your appreciation.

They have Trouble Connecting Emotionally and Communication Difficulties

Research shows that those with this attachment style are less accurate than those with a secure attachment when trying to identify the emotions that others are feeling. When they become stressed, their accuracy becomes even less. As a result, they often misinterpret the behaviors of others or what they say. If your date feels that you are upset when you are not, or they tend to walk away from an argument rather than talking about it, it may be a sign that they have an avoidant attachment style.

They Do Not Communicate Loss

When it comes to loss, be it the death of a loved one or not getting the job they wanted, those with an avoidant attachment style demonstrated the same level of emotions and physiological changes that securely attached individuals do. However, they tended not to verbally express those feelings. Not only did they not verbally express their feelings, but they also suppressed their physiological responses. This was the conclusion of a study by the University of Illinois (Fraley, 2023).

If the person you are dating seems to have a cold or emotionless demeanor after experiencing a loss, it is not because they are resilient. Rather, they have learned to suppress any expressions of vulnerability.

It is for all these reasons that trying to have a relationship with someone who has an avoidant attachment style can be a lonely experience as they will resist allowing the relationship to become meaningful and fulfilling.

When the relationship gets to be serious, they will distance themselves. It is at this point that they will find reasons to break up. This behavior is an expression of how they avoided emotional intimacy with their caregiver.

If someone has an avoidant attachment style, all of these indicators that were just mentioned will be occurring subconsciously. They are reliving their childhood when their caregivers ignored their emotional needs. Their lack of trust in others and the need to care for themselves continues into adulthood. The following is additional information to help better understand them:

Asking for Reassurance

Asking for reassurance from this attachment style may be perceived by them that you are making a huge demand on them. This is because these individuals are extremely vigilant to potential control or manipulation. As children, they learned of the pain that comes from failing their caregivers. After all, why else would their caregivers have distanced themselves from them?

Additionally, they may perceive the request for reassurance as criticism. Finally, avoidant-attached individuals are averse to conflict. They feel threatened discussing any topic that may lead to fighting. Instead, they may behave passive-aggressively and offer you empty promises.

Former Partners

Avoidant attachment styles may maintain contact with ex-partners. They may spend time with them in-person or through social media. Also, they may make their phone off-limits to you. All of this may make you feel like you are their backup plan or that you are competing for their attention.

These individuals use their former partners as a strategy to put you in your place. By doing so, it is hoped that you will feel vulnerable. In turn, your insecurity will make them feel more powerful.

Becoming Their Therapist

Beware of falling for the trap where you give your support to them unconditionally. You may believe that they will become closer to you by doing so. Unfortunately, what usually happens is that it destroys any chance of developing a romantic relationship.

Those with this attachment style treasure friendship over romantic partners. In their minds, the safest way to maintain a relationship with you is to consider you a friend. Though partners with an avoidant attachment style may pull away from the relationship, it does not mean they do not love you.

Avoidant Attachment Style and Triggers

The behaviors of the avoidant attachment style are not demonstrated regularly. As with other attachment styles, the behaviors appear when they are triggered. The dismissive attitude and behaviors that this attachment type engages in are ultimately forms of defense when they feel threatened by separation or loss of a relationship.

When they perceive a threat, some will focus their attention on unrelated issues or their goals. This attachment type will deny their vulnerability, pull away, and attempt to deal with the threat on their own.

When triggered, this attachment type is likely to withdraw and repress their emotions as a way to manage them. At times of crisis, and if they do seek support from their partner, they will be indirect about it. They may resort to sulking, complaining, or hinting.

There are three main triggers that elicit the avoidant behaviors of this attachment style:

- The fear of being taken advantage of.

- The fear of emotional overwhelm.

- The fear of being rejected or abandoned.

The Fear of Being Taken Advantage Of

For those with an avoidance attachment style, maintaining control is of utmost importance. This s one of the reasons why entering a relationship is so scary for them. In their minds, entering a relationship means giving up control. To them, the idea of giving up control to another person means that they would become vulnerable to being exploited or taken advantage of.

Fear of Emotional Overwhelm

For the person with an avoidance attachment style, there is a fear of being overwhelmed by the emotions of another person. They have difficulty managing their own emotions. The idea of taking on the emotions of another is suffocating for them. This is the next reason why individuals with this attachment style retreat from others.

The Fear of Rejection or Abandonment

Many people with insecure attachment styles have suppressed their emotions for years as a way to avoid experiencing their pains. The idea of opening up to another person is very scary for them. Not only would opening up cause them to feel their pain, but they also fear that they will be rejected or abandoned by others. This fear prevents them from forming meaningful connections with others.

Signs that an Avoidant Partner Loves You

It is important to remember that the avoidant behaviors of a person with this attachment style are learned from childhood. They adopted their avoidant behavior for emotional survival. Given this, how can you tell if an avoidant partner loves you? The following are things to look out for:

Nonverbal Signs of Affection

Instead of expressing emotions and affection for their partner, they will demonstrate it in nonverbal ways. These can include affectionate touches, warm smiles, and prolonged eye contact.

Letting Down of Boundaries

As they feel more secure, they may let down their guard and loosen up on their boundaries. It is important to note that relationships go through highs and lows, so they may reestablish their boundaries when there is a down period in the relationship.

Showing Vulnerability

Avoidant partners are uncomfortable with showing vulnerability. If they share their emotions with you, it is a sign that they feel comfortable with you.

Being Responsive to Your Needs

When an avoidant partner is responsive to your needs, it demonstrates that they care about your happiness. When they do so, reinforce them by expressing your appreciation.

Sharing Your Interest

This attachment style has a strong independence streak. If they are willing to get involved with your interests, it may be a sign that they are developing deeper feelings for you.

Wanting to Take it Slow

In a dating relationship, if the avoidant person tells you that they do not want to rush having sex, that is a hopeful sign, as this attachment style tends to be hyper-sexual.

Make Yourself at Home

In the early stages of the relationship, if the avoidant partner leaves you alone in their apartment or home, it is a sign that they trust you. This attachment style is very private, so leaving you in their personal space says a lot.

Going Traveling

This attachment style finds making commitments to be very scary. If they are willing to take a trip with you, that indicates they have serious feelings for you. One word of caution, though, you may want to prepare yourself to be scrutinized by them. They may use the occasion to scrutinize everything you say and do to judge whether there is long-term compatibility.

Willingness to Seek Help

Discussing feelings, being vulnerable, and seeking help are behaviors to which avoidant types have a strong aversion. If your partner is willing to go to therapy, it is a sign that they have strong feelings for you.

Expressions of Endearment

Besides the willingness to seek therapy, another monumental sign that they have strong feelings for you is that they demonstrate acts of service, give you gifts, and engage in physical touch or sex.

Being in A Relationship with Avoidant Partner

If you are in a relationship with someone who has an avoidant attachment style, or you plan to be, there are some important things that you should know so that you can better meet your needs while respecting theirs.

Maintaining a relationship with someone with an avoidant attachment style is very difficult. You will find yourself having to do a balancing act between making your partner feel safe and not compromising your need for intimacy and affection. There are certain rules that you should set for yourself to avoid getting caught up in their attachment style:

Know Your Value as a Person

A big mistake is trying to appease them at your expense. A person with an avoidance attachment style will get bored quickly with those who try to appease them. It is important to know your worth and not turn to them for validation.

Know Your Attachment Style

Because of their unique traits, each of the attachment styles will affect your compatibility with your partner differently. If both partners are of the avoidant style, the compatibility will be high. The partners will respect each other's need for space and discomfort in showing emotions.

A person with an anxious partner is likely to have difficulty understanding the avoidant partner's needs. Understanding your attachment style is invaluable for this reason.

Do not Take it Personally

Regardless of how hard you try to support an avoidant partner; they will need their personal space from time to time. Regardless of how much they value you as a partner, they still need their space.

Set firm Boundaries

Setting boundaries is recommended in any relationship, but it is especially important if you get involved with someone with an avoidant attachment style. You need to know what behaviors you will not tolerate.

Stay True to Your Life

Do not give up on your relationships, hobbies, or interests when getting involved with this attachment style. Of course, this is good advice for any relationship. However, it is especially important for this attachment style. An avoidant partner will dismiss you if you try to pursue a closer connection with them.

Be Clear and Direct

It is important that you are clear, direct, and specific when expressing your needs. If you try to communicate your needs any other way, you will likely get excuses from them.

Do Not Judge

Those with an avoidant attachment easily feel that they are being judged. It is important to them to be able to prove themselves. Avoid saying anything that may sound like you are judging, as that will trigger their attachment style.

Present Them with a Challenge

This is not to imply that you should play games with them. Instead, it is a strategy for getting avoidants to approach you. By being slightly aloof, they will feel more comfortable being with you.

Give Up on Saving Them

You are guaranteed to experience disappointment or heartache if you enter a relationship to fix or save them. The only thing that you can hope for is that you make them feel safe enough that they desire to change themselves.

How to More Effectively Relate to an Avoidant Partner

Those who have an avoidant attachment style have a compelling need for independence and to avoid emotional intimacy. The most compatible person for such an individual is someone who is also very independent. Based on this, the following are suggestions for communicating with an avoidant partner:

Give Them Space

When your partner wants space, do your best to honor their request. Not honoring their request will only make them want to distance themselves even more so. The important thing is not to take their desire for space personally.

Acknowledge Your Differences

Learn to accept that your partner's need for connection and affection may be very different than your own. Understand that just because they do not feel the way they do does not mean that they do not love you.

Encourage Disclosure

Practice active listening when your partner discloses what they are thinking about or what they are feeling. Active listening means being supportive, nonjudgmental, and not trying problem solve. You are compassionately listening to understand what they are trying to say and to allow them to express themselves.

Develop Self-Reliance

Becoming self-reliant is the most effective way to win the trust of an avoidant partner and maintain the relationship. Develop your own interest and nurture yourself by spending time with your friends, engaging in your own interests, and taking time for self-care. By you becoming more self-reliant, your partner may become more open to taking a risk by becoming more emotionally intimate.

Let Go of Unrealistic Expectations

The more you learn about your partner's attachment style, the less likely you will take your partner's behavior personally. Having unrealistic expectations for the relationship will not serve you or your partner.

Communicate Your Needs Successfully

Having an avoidant partner does not mean suppressing how you feel or your needs. Rather, it is learning how to express your feelings and needs in a way that is assertive, clear, and open. If you come across as being emotional, needy, or demanding, it will trigger them.

Accept Your Partner Just the Way They Are

Do not try to fix your partner or try to save them. It is important to remember that your partner is behaving in response to deep-seated patterns that have existed since childhood. It is important to recognize your limitations and that no one is perfect.

Ways to Support Your Avoidant Partner

It is not uncommon for people to change their attachment styles as they grow older or through life experiences. For this reason, it is possible to enjoy a romantic relationship with an avoidant partner if both parties are willing to work on it. Of course, you cannot change them; they need to want to change. The following are suggestions for how you can support your avoidant partner.

Let Them Know Your Motivation

When you do something for your partner, let them know that you wanted to do it for them, not because you felt that they needed help. As stated earlier, avoidants do not want to accept help from others because they feel accepting help indicates weakness or neediness. Additionally, they may become concerned that they are becoming a burden to you and that it will drive you away.

Listen Without Being Judgmental or Being Defensive

Should you reach the point in your relationship when your avoidant partner starts sharing their concerns with you, be careful in the way that you respond. You will need to walk a fine line between giving them assurance that things will work out and not getting caught up in their fears.

Let Me Count the Ways

Express to your avoidant partner all the different ways that you appreciate them. You can do this throughout the day whenever you can think of something sincere to tell them. When expressing your appreciation for them, make your comments plain and simple. Though they may not reciprocate, it will help dispel any doubts that they may have about the relationship.

Make Self-Care a Priority

While providing emotional support to your avoidant partner is important, it is just as important that you care for your own emotional health. Whenever you feel that you may be too demanding of your partner or you feel that you are becoming too needy, take time to take care of yourself. While doing this is important in any relationship, it is especially important in a relationship with an avoidant personality. Consider things like spending time with friends, meditation, or exercise.

If you are truly involved with a person with an avoidant attachment style, you will have a lot of emotional work ahead of you. However, it is not an entirely different game than being in a relationship with someone with a secure attachment style. You are addressing the same areas of concern; it is just that you need to be extra mindful of the way that you do things.

CHAPTER 8

Avoidant Attachment Style and Boundaries

When you hear the word "boundaries," what comes to your mind? For many, that word brings thoughts of creating distance or building walls to protect ourselves from others. In truth, creating boundaries creates liberation, increasing the probability of enjoying a healthy and respectful relationship. More importantly, it reinforces a sense of dignity for us and others.

Instead of creating distance or building walls, boundaries create the foundation for a healthy and thriving relationship. But what are boundaries? Boundaries are rules that we create for ourselves that promote respect for each other. Setting boundaries allows us to feel comfortable in a relationship, and they build self-esteem. These three items, respect, feeling comfortable, and healthy self-esteem, are crucial for a healthy relationship.

Rather than constraining a relationship, boundaries cultivate mutual respect. They allow each person to feel comfortable in the relationship and prevent unnecessary arguments, misunderstandings, or hurt feelings. In relationships, boundaries indicate what each person's limits are.

By understanding each other's limits, we create a relationship where each person can feel respected, comfortable, and safe. Further, the boundaries that you create for yourself are flexible. As the nature of your relationship changes, you can make changes to your boundaries. In short, setting boundaries allows you to be true to who you are.

It is important to note that boundaries are needed in any relationship, regardless of how long you have been together. However, those with an insecure attachment style often have difficulties setting boundaries. In this chapter, we will explore how to implement and respond to boundaries when the avoidant attachment style is involved.

Setting Boundaries

It is never easy to say "no" to someone who you love or care about. Ironically, these are the people for which boundaries are most needed as they are the ones whom we have the most difficulty expressing limits. Boundaries provide clarity within a relationship as to what each partner expects from the other. There are two kinds of boundaries, physical and emotional.

Physical Boundaries

Physical Boundaries involve the space around us and our bodies. These boundaries include unwanted touching and the invasion of personal space. Examples of physical boundaries include:

- Not reading another person's emails or text messages.

- Not entering another person's room without permission.

- Not touching another person when it makes them uncomfortable.

Emotional Boundaries

Establishing emotional boundaries involves communicating what you need to feel safe emotionally. It also involves not letting the moods of others take priority over how you feel. You are not responsible for how others feel. It is important to learn how to respect how others feel while honoring how you feel.

It is important to know what your emotional boundaries are and to communicate them to others. The following are examples of expressing emotional boundaries:

- I appreciate that you want to find solutions to help me, but what I need is for you to just listen to me.

- I do not want to talk about it now. Can we talk about it when it is a better time?

- It is difficult for me to share with you when I feel like you dismiss my feelings.

- I can see that this is a difficult time for you; I think we need to have some space to be alone.

- When you are upset, you take it out on me, and that is not fair.

Healthy versus Unhealthy Boundaries

Healthy boundaries allow you to communicate your wants and needs while at the same time respecting the wants and needs of those around you. Examples of healthy boundaries include:

- Your ability to say "no," and honor the wishes of others when they say "no."

- You have the ability to clearly and assertively communicate your wants and needs.

- You are able to respect and honor your needs and those of others.

- You have the ability to respect the beliefs, opinions, and values of others.

- You have the ability to freely express yourself where it is appropriate.

- You are able to be flexible in your boundaries without compromising yourself.

Unhealthy boundaries result in us feeling emotionally or physically unsafe within the relationship. Examples of unhealthy boundaries include:

- You have difficulty in saying "no" or accepting "no" from others.

- You have difficulty communicating your wants and needs.

- You readily compromise your beliefs, personal values, or opinions to satisfy others.

- You are manipulative or coercive when trying to get others to do things they do not wish to do.

- You disclose too much personal information.

Why Setting Boundaries is Important

When you set boundaries for yourself, you protect yourself from being manipulated or taken advantage of. Further, you strengthen your self-esteem. Additionally, you improve the quality of your relationships because the other person knows what your expectations are. Setting boundaries also improves relationships because they provide you with a safe space to grow and become vulnerable. Relationships thrive when each person can feel safe to be who they are and express themselves, allowing them to grow and move beyond their comfort zone.

When dating, setting boundaries provides clarity in the relationship from the first day. By communicating your boundaries to the other person, they learn what you expect in a relationship. In turn, how they respond to you will let you know if you should continue to see them.

Boundaries and the Attachment Styles

Each of the attachment styles tends to respond to boundaries differently. Those with a secure attachment style tend to understand the importance of boundaries and are respectful of them. Those with an anxious attachment style tend to have more difficulty respecting boundaries and are more likely to violate their partner's need for space.

Those with an avoidant attachment style are more likely to feel that their boundaries have been violated than the other attachment styles, which makes sense because, by nature, they have a tendency to distance themselves emotionally and physically. Because they tend to suppress their emotions, they are less likely to get angry when their boundaries have been intruded upon. Also, when someone with this attachment style intrudes on the boundaries of others, their motivation for doing so is usually out of concern for the other person's well-being.

Things to Consider When Setting Boundaries

The following are suggestions for when setting boundaries with someone who has an avoidant attachment style:

Identify Your Own Need for Boundaries

Take time to reflect on what you need to feel safe, both emotionally and physically, within the relationship. One way you can do this is to think about the behavioral patterns in your current or past relationships that made you feel safe and those that did not. Identify the patterns that supported your bond with your partner. For example, if you need your partner to respect and not dismiss your concerns, that is a boundary that you need to create.

Also, when choosing your boundaries for the relationship, it is important to check in with yourself. Is the boundary something that you need to feel safe in the relationship, or is it an excuse to put up a wall between you and your partner? This can be clarified to yourself by asking yourself what the goal of your boundaries is.

Determine Your Attachment Style

Identifying your attachment style can be helpful when determining what boundaries, you need within the relationship. If you have an avoidant attachment style, you will have less of a need for proximity to your partner than if you had an avoidant attachment style.

Be Honest and Open in Your Communication

Being honest and open with someone you love can be difficult. However, it is the only way to set boundaries. It may be difficult, but not having boundaries that are clearly communicated will more likely lead to relationship issues down the line. To make it easier for you, start small and focus on one boundary at a time. Also, if communicating your boundaries to your partner makes you nervous, write them out and practice saying them in front of a mirror.

When communicating your boundaries, avoid saying "you," as it may sound accusatory. Instead, stay calm and use more "I" statements. Below are examples:

- "I feel_____ when I am spoken to that way."

- "Whenever_____   happens,   I feel_____."

- "I do not appreciate the way that I am being spoken to at this moment."

- "I do want to talk to you about this, but right now, it is not the right time for me.

- "I need more time to think about it, but I will let you know."

- "I would like to help you, but right now, I have too much going on."

It is a Two-Way Street

While you have your relationship needs, your partner has their own. Further, they may not understand what those needs are, let alone how to express them to you. It is important that you and your partner learn to communicate with each other in an open and nonjudgmental way. By doing this, you will have taken a big step toward a more balanced and healthier relationship.

CHAPTER 9

Avoidant Attachment Style and the Power of Mindfulness

This book has provided a wide range of suggestions for how to cope with an avoidant attachment style. In most cases, working with a therapist will be the most effective way to learn how to manage the way the thoughts and behaviors that are associated with this attachment style.

The reason for this is that the thoughts and behaviors of this attachment style are deeply rooted within the person. Learning to overcome these tendencies involves awareness and overcoming a great deal of resistance from within ourselves. There is, however, a powerful way to assist you in creating a healthier attachment style, which is through the practice of mindfulness.

Running on Autopilot

Have you ever misplaced something, like your car keys, and were unable to find them? Perhaps, you gave up looking for them, or you got distracted by something. Either way, you returned to your normal activities. Then, sure enough, you find your keys! You find them in a place where you failed to look, or you find them out in the open. You just did not see them while searching.

Why did you not find your keys when you were searching for them? The answer to that question is simple; you were not being mindful. Here is another example. Have you ever walked into a room and forgot why you entered it? I am sure you have, as we have all done this. Why did we do this? It is the same answer; we were not being mindful.

These are just two examples of how we become caught up in thought, which keeps us from experiencing the present moment. Most of our thoughts involve the future or the past. The thoughts that we have of the past are our memories. The thoughts that we have of the future are our anticipations. Because we spend so much time caught up in the past and the future, our attention is not on what is happening in the present moment. It is for this reason that we cannot find our car keys or why we forget our reasons for entering the room.

So, what does mindfulness have to do with an avoidant

attachment style or another insecure form of attachment? Those who have an avoidant attachment style are often focused on the memories of their past or their fears of what may happen in the future.

We continue to operate by the same kind of thinking that we have operated from for most of our lives. Our thoughts, feelings, and actions are recycled from the past. In other words, we are operating from autopilot. Because we are operating from past thoughts, we have the same anticipations of what will happen in the future, which is why we feel triggered.

What has just been described is true for all of us, whether we have an avoidant attachment or not. At a conscious level, we believe that we have free choice in how we will respond to a situation. While we have the capacity to do so, most of us are not operating from free choice. Rather, we are following the habitual thoughts and patterns of behavior that have guided us in the past. It is only when we extend our awareness beyond our habitual thinking that we can experience the present moment in a way that has not been tainted by the memories of our past or our anticipation of the future.

What is Mindfulness?

Mindfulness is nothing more than awareness. To be aware is to be aware of what is being experienced at the moment. The practice of mindfulness dates back 2,500 years but has not been practiced on a societal level for a long time. Only recently has mindfulness regained popularity.

Have you ever seen a magnificent sunset or other natural wonder? Do you remember what it was like to hold your child for the first time? Can you recall what it was like when you spent time being with the person who you were in love with? We have all experienced moments like these, moments where we felt fully present. We were not caught up in our thinking. During these moments, we felt alive and complete. We experienced moments of stillness where we were not caught up in our plans or worries. These are the moments where we were fully present, though perhaps just momentarily.

The Nature of Thought

Most of the time, we are not mindful. Instead of being fully present, we are caught up in our thoughts. When we get caught up in our thoughts, we cannot be present. The reason for this has to do with our relationship with our thoughts. We often personalize our thoughts, meaning that we take on their identity. If we have angry thoughts, we become angry. If we have worrisome thoughts, we become worried, and if we have loving thoughts, we become loving. When we personalize our thoughts, they become the lens through which we experience reality. This is particularly true when it comes to our beliefs.

Beliefs are thoughts about which we have a sense of certainty about. In other words, we believe them to be true. Our beliefs determine what we focus on and how we respond to a situation. If you believe that you cannot do something, you will focus on all the reasons why you cannot do it. Because of this, your response will be consistent with your beliefs. You will not give your best effort, or you may not even try.

Now, try this simple exercise:

1. Sit or lie down, close your eyes, and relax.

2. As you relax further, visualize a beautiful sunset. Visualize it with as much detail as possible. Note: Everyone visualizes, though this ability varies from person to person. Some people can see their visualizations in vivid detail, while the visualizations of others can be very vague or faint. This does not matter. Just make your visualization as real as possible according to your ability.

3. Now visualize a black cat and see it as vividly as possible.

4. Lastly, visualize a full moon. Again, make it as real as possible.

5. Now open your eyes.

During this visualization exercise, you visualized a beautiful sunset, a black cat, and a full moon. At no time did you confuse yourself with any of these visualizations? You knew that you were not the sunset, the black cat, or the full moon; you were the observer of these things. These visualizations were just thoughts that took on a visual dimension.

You did not identify with these thoughts. The reason for this is that these thoughts were not considered as being important by your mind, so you did not identify with them.

When you practice mindfulness, you will be less likely to personalize your beliefs, so you will be less likely to run on autopilot. You will be able to evaluate the situation and respond in an empowering way. The following is an example:

Greg has an avoidant attachment style. His partner is feeling frustrated and wants to talk to him about it. As Greg listens, he experiences uneasy feelings as he senses that it is going to lead to an argument. Greg's natural instincts kick in, and Greg emotionally closes down to protect himself. He then leaves the room, which leaves his partner feeling unheard.

The reason why Greg shut down was because he identified with the thoughts that he was experiencing. His thoughts and beliefs were telling him that experiencing his emotions, or the emotions of his partner, would lead to a negative outcome.

It is important to point out that we not only identify with our thoughts, but we also identify with our emotions. Our attachment styles are based on beliefs that we do not question and with which we identify. As you experienced in the previous exercise, it is possible to have thoughts and not identify with them.

If Greg practiced mindfulness, he would have an awareness of the thoughts and emotions that were arising from within him. Further, he would not judge what he was thinking or feeling. He would be accepting of their existence and allow them to present themselves without identifying with them.

Because Greg would not be identifying with his thoughts and feelings, he would be able to evaluate whether they accurately reflect what is happening in the situation with his partner.

Mindfulness Exercises

The following exercises will help you cultivate mindfulness. The more you practice these exercises, the more skillful you will become in becoming mindful. As you develop your mindfulness skills, your awareness of what you are experiencing will become more expansive.

Mindful Breathing

The following exercise will allow you to develop the ability to slow down your thoughts and increase the power of your awareness.

1. Find a place to sit down, making sure that you are comfortable. Try to find a place that offers solitude and is free of distractions. With practice, you will be able to practice in almost any kind of environment, regardless of the distractions that may exist.

2. Close your eyes and allow yourself to relax. Breathing normally, place your attention on the flow of your breath through your nose. Focus on the sensations that you experience as you inhale and exhale. Notice the sensation of your breath as you inhale. Experience the sensations of air entering your nasal cavity and your chest and abdomen rising. When exhaling, notice the sensations in your abdomen and chest falling and that of the air leaving your nasal cavity.

3. Continue to observe the flow of breath as it courses through your body. Feel yourself become more and more relaxed with each breath you take.

4. As you practice this technique, you are bound to experience your mind wandering as you get distracted by thoughts. As soon as you are aware that this has happened, gently redirect your focus back to your breath. Do not judge yourself when losing your concentration,

regardless of how often this happens. The more you practice, the more you will be able to maintain your concentration without being distracted.

5. Similarly, if you experience distracting sensations or emotions, do not judge these either. Simply accept these distractions without trying to change or avoid them and continue to focus on your breath.

The goal of mindful practice is to become aware of thoughts, emotions, and sensations without getting involved with them. With continued practice, you will discover that these phenomena of the mind and body are not who you are; they are objects of the mind, and you are the one who is aware of them.

Mindfulness of the Sensations of the Body

Our body experiences innumerable sensations, yet we are so distracted in our daily lives we often are unaware of them. This mindfulness exercise will help you develop greater awareness of your body's sensations.

1. Lie down on the floor or a mat (Using your bed for this exercise is discouraged as you may fall asleep.

2. Place your attention on the movement of your breath as you inhale and exhale.

3. As you follow your breath, become aware of the sensations of your body. Do you detect a tingling in your feet or hands? Do you sense pressure or stiffness in your back, shoulders, or neck? Allow yourself to experience every sensation that you are aware of. Do not try to change them, ignore them, or judge them as being good or bad. Simply allow yourself to experience them.

4. Notice that the sensations you feel are not stable as they constantly change in their degree of intensity, while some may seem to appear, disappear, and then reappear.

5. Allow yourself to experience any given sensation for as long as you desire. When you are ready, just move on to another sensation.

6. Be sure to continue breathing as you perform this exercise.

7. Continue to practice this exercise as long as you wish.

Relaxation

Progressive relaxation is an exercise that relieves stress and promotes relaxation by sequentially tightening the body's muscles. Besides relaxing the body and developing greater awareness of the body's sensations, doing this exercise before going to bed can be helpful if you have trouble sleeping.

1. Lie down in bed and allow yourself to relax and be comfortable.

2. Focus on your breathing for a few minutes, paying attention to your breath as it travels through your body during inhalation and exhalation.

3. Close your eyes and breathe. Notice how your abdomen rises and falls as your breath flows in and out.

4. Feel the relaxation in your body as you breathe.

5. When you exhale, pay attention to the sensations in your body. Do you feel more relaxed?

6. Curl your toes. Hold it for a few seconds, and then relax. Feel the sensation of relaxation.

7. Tighten your thighs. Hold it for a few seconds, and then relax. Feel the sensation of relaxation. As you breathe out, feel your legs becoming heavier and more relaxed.

8. Tighten the muscles of the buttocks, hold them for a few seconds, and then relax. Feel the sensation of relaxation.

9. Tighten the muscles of your abdomen. Hold it for a few seconds, and then relax. Feel the sensation of relaxation.

10. Take three deep breaths using your diagram. As you inhale, focus on your abdomen rising. When exhaling,

focus on your abdomen falling. After taking three deep breaths, inhale for a fourth breath and hold it. Hold your breath for as long as you can. When you exhale, focus on the sensations of the body as the air is released from your body.

11. Raise your shoulders toward your ears, raising them as high as possible. Hold it for a few seconds, and then relax. Feel the sensation of relaxation.

12. Tilt your head back as far as possible. Hold it for a few seconds, and then relax. Feel the sensation of relaxation.

13. Raise your head toward your chest. Hold it for a few seconds, and then relax. Feel the sensation of relaxation.

14. Tighten your jaw. Hold it for a few seconds, and then relax. Feel the sensation of relaxation.

15. Raise your brow as high as possible. Hold it for a few seconds, and then relax. Feel the sensation of relaxation.

16. Tighten your brow as much as possible. Hold it for a few seconds, and then relax. Feel the sensation of relaxation.

17. Take time just to relax and enjoy the sensations of your body.

Mindfulness of the Walking

Mindfulness can be practiced anywhere and at any time, as it involves being aware of what is being experienced at the moment. The following is an exercise for walking in mindfulness.

1. When first practicing this exercise, it helps to start with designating a short distance (approximately ten feet) in which you will practice mindful walking. You can extend the distance as you get more comfortable with this exercise.

2. With your route marked out, walk the distance of your route at a relaxed pace. As you walk, place your awareness on the sensation of the sole of your shoes as they contact the ground. Make sure as you are walking that you continue to breathe.

3. As you become more skillful in focusing on the sensations of walking, you can extend your awareness of what is happening in your environment. Listen to the sound of birds singing, the wind blowing, the sound of cars, or the sound of people talking. As always in mindful practice, do not judge, analyze, or evaluate anything you experience; your only job is to be aware.

Mindfulness in Eating

Have you ever eaten while watching television or talking to

someone, then realized that you have consumed your meal without any memory of doing so? Perhaps you realized that you ate your meal but had no memory of really tasting it? When we eat this way, we are not mindful of our eating. As a matter of fact, many problems with digestion or maintaining our proper weight are due, in part, to not eating mindfully. When we are not eating mindfully, we deny ourselves savoring our food as our minds are elsewhere.

When practicing mindful eating, it is important to set up your environment so that you will not be distracted as you eat. You can eat alone or find someone who would be interested in eating mindfully with you, meaning there is to be no conversation while eating. Also, turn off all electronic devices and ensure you have everything you need to enjoy your meal, so you do not have to get up to get something while eating. Lastly, it is recommended that you eat a healthy meal. As the purpose of practicing mindfulness is mental well-being, you also want to enjoy physical health.

1. Take time to relax and focus on your breath. Allow yourself to relax.

2. When you are ready, look at your food, and observe its color, shape, and texture.

3. Take in its aroma. How does your food smell? Is its aroma weak, mild, or strong?

4. Now taste your food but do so mindfully. Take only bite-size pieces and take your time before swallowing them. Allow yourself to savor its taste and how it feels in your mouth.

5. When you are ready, swallow your food.

Showering Mindfully

How many times have you taken a shower, only to realize while your body was in the shower, your mind was elsewhere? You can practice mindfulness in everything you do, and showering is no different. Taking a shower mindfully is a great way to become more in touch with your body, its sensations, and awareness of the present moment.

When taking a shower, you want your full attention on the experience of taking a shower, not on your memories or your thoughts of the future. Your only job is to take in all the sensory experiences of taking a shower. It is only natural that thoughts will arise while taking a shower, which is okay. Do not react to your thoughts; ignore them and return your attention to the sensation of taking a shower. Allow yourself to experience whatever is happening at that moment.

As you take your shower, place your focus on what you are experiencing. Here are some examples:

- Place your attention on the feelings of the water running down your body.

- Feel the sensation of the water against your skin.

- Listen to the sound of your breath.

- Listen to the sound of the water cascading downward.

- Smell the shampoo or soap that you are using.

- Feel the sensations of the soles of your feet on the shower floor.

- Feel the sensations as you work the shampoo into your hair.

- Watch as the water glides down your body.

- Watch the water as it flows down the shower drain.

- Watch the water drops splatter as they contact the shower floor.

Mindful Observing

Find a place that is comfortable for you. It can be indoors or outdoors. Sit down and allow yourself to relax. For the next 10 minutes, simply observe everything around you. Observe what you experience from within yourself (i.e., thoughts, emotions, sensations, or feelings).

Whatever it is that you notice, do not judge, evaluate, or analyze it. You are just to observe it. Feel free to go longer if you wish. Practice this each day, increasing the observation time each day. When doing this exercise, you should stay relaxed. You cannot get this exercise wrong. Even if you judge, allow yourself to experience this without judgment.

CHAPTER 10

Can Your Attachment Style Change Over Time?

Can you change your attachment style? The answer to that question appears to be "no" and "yes." The literature appears to agree that we cannot change from one style to another; however, we can alter our attachment style to become more or less secure. The following are three scenarios that illustrate how a life situation can change one's attachment style:

Scenario 1:

A child grows up in a loving and supportive home and develops a secure attachment style. Having a secure attachment style, he learns to trust others and is comfortable with emotional intimacy.

When he gets older, he starts to date. Unfortunately, he experiences a series of disappointing and unhealthy relationships. His partners have insecure attachment styles. They cheat on him, lie to him, or monitor his communications on his social media accounts and cell phones.

Repeated relationships of this kind destroy his confidence, resulting in him adopting a more insecure attachment style. He moves toward the avoidant end of the attachment style spectrum.

Scenario 2:

A woman has an anxious attachment style and is in a relationship where she always feels like she is on shaky ground. She forever fears that her partner will leave or that he is cheating on her. The relationship eventually breaks up. Tired of living this way, she gets therapy and works on herself.

Her efforts pay off, and she meets someone new. Her relationship with her new partner is more characteristic of a secure attachment style. She rarely experiences feelings of anxiousness or jealousy. When she does, she knows how to deal with it healthily.

Scenario 3:

A man has an anxious attachment style. Because of this, his relationships are characterized by the constant need for validation from his partners. He decides to go to therapy and spends a lot of time working on himself. Later, he enters a new relationship. He eventually realizes his partner has an insecure attachment style. Instead of reverting to his anxious attachment style, he interacts with his partner more securely.

Research also shows that attachments may change over time as we get older. It is theorized that as we get older, we tend to have a lower tolerance for relationships that do not meet our needs as we have less time (PsychCentral, 2022).

The Research: It Does Not Take Much!

Studies have shown that a change in attachment style can occur through positive experiences of closeness and intimacy (Jackson, 2021). One study involved 70 heterosexual couples who participated in a survey regarding their relationship. The couples were then placed into two groups. The first group engaged in activities that promoted greater intimacy and closeness.

These couples took turns answering a series of questions about themselves. The questions selected by the researchers had been proven to enhance feelings of closeness. Another activity this group got involved in was partner yoga, a form of yoga that involved holding hands or other forms of physical contact while creating poses.

The second group engaged in activities that involved answering impersonal questions and individual yoga. After completing their exercises, the participants assessed the quality of their relationships.

Those in the first group, who were identified as having an avoidant style, rated the quality of their relationship higher than they did before participating in the activities. Those who were identified as having a secure or anxious attachment style did not show any change in how they perceived their relationship. This study appears to show that activities that build intimacy may be a benefit for those with an avoidant attachment style.

What is remarkable is that there was a follow-up on the participants one month later. The increase in satisfaction that the avoidant style participants reported was still there (Jackson, 2021). The study also revealed that similar results occurred in couples engaged in spontaneous home interactions. In this study, 67 heterosexual couples in a long-term relationship were asked to keep a diary every day for three weeks. They were told to record their feelings and their partner's behavior toward them (Jackson, 2021)

The study's results found that when the romantic partners of the participants behaved positively toward them, they experienced positive emotions more frequently and negative ones less frequently. They were also happier about their relationship. Positive behaviors by the romantic partners included loving behaviors and listening to the other partner.

These findings were most evident in participants with an avoidant attachment. These studies suggest that those with an avoidant attachment style are more likely to benefit from a positive relationship than those with other insecure styles.

What is encouraging about these studies is that they show that a shift to a more secure attachment style can take place by taking action that involves little time or effort. In another study, it was found that those with an avoidant attachment style could reduce the magnitude of their negative emotions by just reflecting on positive relationship memories (Jackson, 2021).

The goal of those with an anxious attachment style should be to become more responsible for themselves. It is recommended that they engage in self-care and learn to nurture themselves. Also important is that they learn to take things slow when dating.

Those who are avoidant would do well to become more attentive to their partner's needs. It would be valuable for them to reveal their vulnerability, acknowledge their need for love, learn to receive, and set their boundaries verbally. Working on these things will cultivate a more secure and interdependent relationship.

It is important to point out that creating change for both insecure attachment styles mean facing the fear of becoming dependent on someone. This is especially true after ending a codependent relationship. However, such fears normally come from being in a codependent relationship where neither partner has a secure attachment. A healthy form of dependency leads to greater interdependence by entering a secure relationship.

The fear of becoming dependent on another can also arise when seeking therapy. In this case, it is the fear of becoming dependent on the therapist. If you experience this, you would be wise to address this fear with your therapist, as this would be a teaching moment to learn how to manage your fear.

Addressing the fear of dependency with a therapist offers the opportunity to develop the skills needed to handle such situations if they arise in the future with a partner. It is here that the paradox lies. Rather than become more dependent, quality therapy can help the individual develop a more secure attachment style, leading to greater autonomy. The greater the autonomy, the more able we will be able to become emotionally intimate with others.

Final Words

One of the most important things to understand about the avoidant attachment style is that it is not some mental illness or disorder. It is a learned way of thinking and behaving. We can think of the avoidant style and the other attachment styles as being a language. We all grew up learning a certain language. Unless we have a secure attachment style, the language we grew up with no longer serves us. We need to learn a new language to live a happier and more fulfilling life.

Using language as a metaphor for attachment styles is also valuable for my next point. Just as whom we are is not defined by the language we speak; our attachment style does not define who we are as individuals. You are not your attachment style. Rather, your attachment style shapes how you think and behave within certain moments of your relationships. I hope this book motivates you to make the necessary changes so that you may live the life you deserve.

References

Cassidy, J., Jones, D. J., and Shaver, R. P. (2013). "Contributions of Attachment Theory and Research: A Framework for Future Research, Translation, and Policy." National Library of Medicine.

Catlett, J. (2022). "Avoidant Attachment: Understanding Insecure Avoidant Attachment," Psychalive.

Edward, E. (2017). "Mary Ainsworth's Strange Situation." Psychology Unlocked.com

Frankenhuis, E. W., (2010). "Did Insecure Attachment Styles Evolve for the Benefit of the Group?" Frontiers in Psychology.

Fraley, C.R. (2023). Adult Attachment Theory and Research. University of Illinois.

Hazen, C. and Shaver, S. (1987). "Romantic Love Conceptualized as an Attachment Process," *Journal of Personality and Social Psychology* Vol. 52.

Hazen, C. and Shaver, P.R., (1990) "Love and Work: An Attachment-Theoretical Perspective,"

Journal of Personality and Social Psychology Vol. 59

Jackson, K., (2021) "Can Your Attachment Style Change? A Therapist Explains."Mindbodygreen.

Lavy, S., Bareli, Y., and Ein-Dor, T. (2014). Team Functioning The Effects of Attachment Heterogeneity and Team Cohesion on. Research Gate.

Li, P. (2022). "Strange Situation Experiment | Ainsworth | Attachment Styles", Parenting for Brain.

MacWilliam, B. (2022). "What is Avoidant Attachment in Relationships? (Traits & Triggers)." Briana MacWilliam website.
McLeod, S., (2017). "Attachment Theory." SimplyPsychology

PsychCentral (2022) "Anxious in Relationships? You Could Change Attachment Styles."

WebMD (2021) "What Is Avoidant Attachment?"

Printed in the USA
CPSIA information can be obtained
at www.ICGtesting.com
LVHW040719290224
773144LV00004B/44

9 781959 750284